| Getting Started |

WITH

JAZZ/SHOW CHOIR

Edited by Russell L. Robinson

Music Educators National Conference

Copyright © 1994

Music Educators National Conference

1806 Robert Fulton Drive, Reston, VA 22091-4348

All rights reserved.

Printed in the United States of America.

ISBN 1-56545-044-2

Contents

Preface v

1. Why Have Jazz/Show Choirs? 1

2. Recruitment and Auditions 5

3. Vocal Health and Production 9

4. Rehearsal Techniques 11

5. Repertoire 15

6. Accompaniment and Sound Equipment 19

7. Choreography 21

8. Shows, Concerts, and Festivals 29

9. Administration 33

10. Outfits 39

Selected Resources 41

Acknowledgments 43

Preface

Jazz/Show choirs have been with us in music education for quite some time. Earlier groups were often called "swing choirs." The distinction between jazz choirs and show choirs is the use or nonuse of choreography and the selection of repertoire; however, the separation is not always clear, nor does it need to be. This book is designed to assist music educators in starting and maintaining jazz/show choirs. The chapter titles reflect what music educators need to know to begin ensembles and instruction in this area. The bottom line in any choral ensemble is high-quality singing, regardless of style. Although show choirs may use staging, microphones, and choreography, the quality of the singing is most important.

This book has some of the best names in the business as contributing authors. This effort by MENC to produce a resource in the jazz/show choir area reflects the philosophy that jazz/show choirs are legitimate ensembles "if they are done legitimately." These busy professionals were willing to make this contribution, and MENC is grateful for their work.

Whether you are looking for assistance in recruiting, holding auditions, facilitating good vocal production, choosing repertoire, selecting outfits, or planning choreography, we hope this book will be a valuable resource for you and your students.

—Russell L. Robinson, Editor

Chapter 1

Why Have Jazz/Show Choirs?

Jazz/Show choirs can and should be an integral part of all outstanding choral programs. The jazz/show choir, when placed in a proper perspective, will be an asset to a balanced program. In such a program, there is no choir that dominates the choral program. This choir should have the same standing as the other choirs.

Many successful choral music programs have been built when new students first become interested in the pizzaz and excitement of a show choir. Following immersion in this choral ensemble, the students learn that the hard work, enthusiasm, and fun in a show choir can be transferred to any choir. Successful choral directors use the same techniques of choral balance, blend, support, and intonation with their jazz/show choirs that they use with their top concert choirs. An outstanding jazz/show choir supplements concert-choir techniques with choreography and exuberance.

Jazz/Show choirs are an excellent vehicle for tapping into high school students' abundant energy. Through dance, they can learn better coordination and confidence. Through learning music and developing their voices, students feel good about themselves, which is very important during the teenage years. The messages that songs leave with students can carry great importance throughout their lives.

The jazz/show choir not only serves as a valuable recruiting ensemble for your total choral program; it also serves as a valuable public-relations tool. The jazz/show choir can create an extensive amount of positive press. Clean-cut, all-American high school students singing their way into the hearts of district patrons will impress the school administration.—RW

Why have a jazz/show choir in your curriculum? Simply put, it is educational from a cultural perspective, and it is an avenue for growth both musically and personally. Show choirs allow students the opportunity to learn the value of community service and allow you to build support for your overall program and reinforce educationally sound principles. By placing the show choir in the curriculum, the status of this ensemble is elevated beyond a club or recreational activity, and we music educators are guaranteed the opportunity to present contemporary music that is an alternative to what our students listen to on radio and television.

Choose challenging music as your show choir grows, demand the students' best effort, and you can and will have a program that is solid, musical, fun, and enriching.—GM

A Place in the Curriculum

The jazz/show choir should and must be placed in the curricular day. The jazz/show choir is equal to all other choral ensembles. It can and will fit easily into an outstanding high school's curriculum.

The school administration must realize that the jazz/show choir is an important part of a choral music program. It is unfair to the students and the director to make this choir rehearse outside of school time. Rehearsing before or after school places an unfair burden on students who don't have their own transportation; such students may not be able to participate.—RW

Do jazz choirs have a place in the school music programs? Yes. There should be a variety of choral groups in the program, including jazz choir.

Jazz is a unique American art form; its very nature is rooted in the idea that music is a creative aural art where performance and improvisation are essential to the experience. In fact a performance without creative interpretation and improvisation has not captured the essence of the genre.

Also, vocal jazz styles and performance practices represent the musical heritages of various cultural and ethnic groups. If a choral curriculum is broad and inclusive rather than exclusive, jazz choirs should be an exciting part of every contemporary music education program. Performing in a jazz choir can and should be a most thrilling and aesthetic experience.

The reason for excluding jazz choirs from the total music program may be found in a lack of training and instruction in jazz at the postsecondary level. Most choral directors come through college and university training programs that focus on liturgical music and Western art music. Jazz choral music is generally not a part of traditional training. There is now a recognized need for more and better vocal jazz courses in university music curricula, as well as vocal jazz workshops or clinics that will meet the needs of contemporary music educators.—DR

Establishing Long-Range Plans and Goals

Every successful choral music program is headed by a director who believes in long-range plans and goals. The goals and plans should include many areas. Here is a partial list: recruitment of students, selection of quality literature, selection of an outfit, and choice of an excellent choreographer who understands the level of the choir, challenges them with new ideas, and enhances the music with exciting movements. The director must impress on the choreographer that the ensemble is a choir, not a dance ensemble that sings.

Additional goals and plans should include performances, festivals, and contests. The best choirs grow with the right amount of performances, and the worst destroy themselves with too many performances. Remember that the students attend school to gain an education, not for the sole purpose of performing in a jazz/show choir.

The most vital and important goal for any show choir is: Be the best possible choir you can be with the "Three T's." The Three T's are time, talent, and treasure. The teacher must create the finest choir possible utilizing the time as scheduled by the administration, the talent available, and the treasure or money available. No teacher can try to make his or her goals greater than the time permitted, talent available, and treasure allocated.—RW

Here are some sample goals:
- Build a vocal jazz library of two-, three-, and four-part arrangements.
   a. Start with easy to moderately difficult pieces.
   b. Select pieces that represent straight-ahead and medium swing, bossa nova, samba, and ballads.
- Develop a repertoire of standard solo literature that includes ballads, blues, swing, bebop, gospel, and Latin styles.
- Learn how to sing jazz articulations.
- Learn how to improvise.
- Learn how to use microphones.
- Learn how to perform as an ensemble using sound vocal techniques.
- Learn how to develop a concert program that has audience appeal.
- Learn how to stage the performance including the positioning of the accompanist, rhythm, and/or horn players. Learn how to use lighting.
- Never stop learning: there is always more to know.

Resolve to:
- listen to jazz from a historical point of view
- learn the standard literature by listening to vocal and instrumental jazz
- broaden your horizons beyond one period or style of jazz
- learn jazz theory, improve your ear and your perception of time
- analyze and transcribe jazz solos
- if possible, attend jam sessions with a jazz musician, notice how a tune is started and ended and how improv solos are managed, especially if the piece being performed is a "head arrangement" (that is, made up on the spot).

- Build a listening library for your students. Jazz is traditionally an aural art, therefore it is necessary to develop aural skills that can be transferred to performance skills.
- Learn about the rhythm section and know the role of each player. Learn about the horn section and techniques for balancing sound volume with the choir (for example, the use of mutes). Enlist the assistance of the instrumental director or a local professional jazz musician.
- Learn about sound systems that can be used with the singers and instrumentalists.

As the show choir gets underway, you will find the blues and jazz mediums to be extremely challenging. These musical forms will fortify, require, and reinforce every technical skill you have ever taught your concert choir. Many texts offer great insights to the human situation in a given time, relationship, or economic or cultural situation. This is great educational material considering the multicultural nation we live in.

Show choirs give the opportunity to reintroduce our students to their parents and grandparents by performing the music of earlier periods. A history lesson can be tied to the big band era or mid-1960s, and the memories evoked in the elder relatives when they see and hear their children and grandchildren perform will bring the past back to them.—DR

Chapter 2
Recruitment and Auditions

Recruitment

The recruitment and audition process for a jazz/show choir is the single most important step in organizing such an ensemble. It is the first of many steps and if the first step is not in the right direction, you may never get back on the right path.

First, I think that this ensemble should require a year-long commitment. At the high school level, it simply isn't possible to develop the necessary skills among your singers in one semester. In order to maximize the success of your group, plan on having the same students together for the entire year. You wouldn't change the personnel of your concert choir each semester—don't do it with your show choir either.

Recruiting for this type of ensemble is fairly easy. What is not easy is finding students insightful enough to understand what a year-long commitment means. I suggest you compose a list of expectations and give each recruit a copy before auditions occur. This list should include all attendance expectations, financial obligations (for example, buying shoes), grading procedures, and concert and festival goals.

You could provide a contract that both student and parent must sign before students are allowed to audition. This contract provides two things; it informs students that you are serious about this group, and it protects you from disgruntled parents who may hit you later with the "I was not informed" position. This process will give you insight as to who is and who isn't really interested.

If you are just starting out, the selection of responsible students is so important. At some point you will have to demonstrate the success of your group to warrant your administrator's continued approval of the program and his or her confidence in you. You, not the students, will be held accountable for the success or failure of a program. Although there are no guarantees, your best hope for success lies in the students you select; therefore, place responsibility among the top characteristics in students you choose.

I place a large emphasis on the audition process. Even if you are just beginning and have to take whatever and whoever you can get, I urge you to develop and require an audition. This sets the tone for years to come and establishes your expectation of this group. It will also give you valuable insight as to the strengths and weaknesses of your personnel.—GM

Auditions

The audition can be a broad and lengthy process. I view it as a test of each student's desire to be in the group and of his or her responsibility, as well as a measure of singing and dancing abilities. Sample audition requirements are as follows:

- Sing solo of contemporary nature (no rap).
- Learn your vocal part, in a group setting, of two pieces of music selected by the director.
- Learn choreography, as taught by the director or assistant, of pieces of music selected by the director.
- Sing your part in selected small groupings.

It's a good idea to hold auditions at the end of each school year to determine the next year's group. This allows you the summer to select and obtain music and think about your teaching approach in this ensemble.

One other note: do not limit yourself to SATB voicing. You may find that you have some girls or guys who do very well together. Be flexible and versatile. You will enjoy it and you can involve more students.—GM

At our institution we hold auditions for vocal jazz ensembles during the first week of classes in the fall. Auditions consist of the following aspects:

- Two contrasting vocal selections.
- Sight-reading.
- Ear-training exercises.
- Vocal improvisation.
- A twenty-four-hour piece (a selection of choral music that auditioners pick up twenty-four hours before the audition. It allows us to see how quickly students can learn a choral part even if they aren't great sight-readers).
- An interview.
- A form that tells us a great deal about a student's attitude and desire to be part of the program.—SZ

Jazz/show choir auditions can be as competitive as a highly publicized cheerleading audition or as quiet as the selection of the third-hour hall monitor. The teacher must carefully plan the audition procedure so it is fair, just, and precise. When the audition criteria are formulated using a point system, each student can receive specific feedback and understand what he or she can do to improve.

A twofold audition procedure has worked at my school. The first part of the audition is with the director of the ensemble, and the second part is with team of "experts." These experts could be teachers you regard highly and who share your philosophy.

For the first round—ten minutes per student—we use the following criteria:

10 points—solo (pitch)
10 points—solo (tone)
10 points—sight-reading (pitch accuracy)
10 points—sight-reading (rhythm)
10 points—choral pitch accuracy
10 points—choral rhythm
10 points—pitch memory

70 total possible points

Prior to the audition date, the director teaches a new show choir selection to all students who desire to audition. Each student signs up for an audition. The teacher hears each student sing for ninety seconds. One to ten points are available for the pitch on the solo that he or she chooses, and one to ten points are available for tone. For the next part of the audition, the student sight-reads a simple twenty-note melody. The director permits the student to see the melody for one minute, gives the first pitch, and asks him or her to sing the melody as accurately as possible. (This is done a cappella.) One-half point is given for each correct pitch (ten possible points), and one-half point is given for each correct rhythm (ten possible points).

The third aspect is the performance of sixty seconds of the new choral selection. The students perform this in quartets or small groups. Each student receives from one to ten points for pitch accuracy and from one to ten points for correct rhythms.

The fourth part tests pitch memory. The director has three tonal memory examples, two that are three notes long and one that is four notes long. The teacher plays each example twice and then asks the student to sing the example on "la." One point is given for each correct pitch. The students with the most points in each section are invited to the final round.

For the second round, the director creates a team of qualified judges. The students sing the new choral selection in quartets. The panel of judges continues blending quartets until they have heard each person several times. Following this the judges cast secret ballots to select the finest singers.

The second audition may also test dance ability. I do not recommend this if the jazz/show choir is a new organization, because it may discourage some talented singers who haven't had dance training.

I recommend that you select alternates in the initial audition, so that if some students must leave the group after one semester, there are others to take their places.—RW

Chapter 3
Vocal Health and Production

How to Sing Styles Correctly

Good vocal production habits depend on keeping the body healthy. When the body is fit and well rested, it is relatively easy to sing properly.

Sound vocal technique is necessary to sing jazz and pop music well. To produce vocal inflections and timbre changes, the singer must be able to sing with a relaxed throat and jaw. Supporting and articulating the air with proper diaphragmatic breathing techniques is equally important.

I like to use this analogy: "Singing jazz or pop music is tantamount to sing a legato line filled with subtle explosions." All jazz styles require the singer to articulate gentle and strong accents. These accents are best achieved by using a very slight inward "tap" with the upper abdominal muscle. For this technique, imagine that you are blowing out five birthday candles in succession with one breath. Keep in mind that you are effecting subtle explosions, not heavy accents.

If this technique is executed properly, there will be no tension in the throat or jaw. To put this technique into practice, you may wish to excerpt a rhythmic motif from the music using scat syllables such as "boo," "dat," "dah," and "dit." Then add the lyrics to your motif. Always apply the sound learning principle of "whole to part to whole."

There is a another problem related to breathing: performing full-voice, forte attacks and energized releases causes some vocalists to press downward for the necessary breath support when they should feel a sustained inward-upward lift in the abdominal area. Pressing downward causes the vocal folds to lock together tightly, and this is the opposite of what the singer needs to do. Furthermore, if this practice is allowed to continue, it will cause extreme vocal fatigue and a hard, raspy sound.

To correct this problem, have the singer use the "birthday candle technique" with one modification. Sustain the air flow on the fifth candle by creating an inward-upward feeling of the abdominal muscles. Put this technique into musical practice by excerpting motifs from the music. Complete the process by putting the properly performed motif back into its musical context.—DR

Vocal Timbre and Vowel Modification

The sound that I enjoy in soloists and vocal jazz or pop groups is a warm resonant timbre enhanced by an even vibrato. I feel every singer should develop the ability to create sound-quality changes when called for—expressive sound is what music is all about. We must remember that jazz has its roots in African music, where timbre and rhythm are the two most critical elements for expression.

Singers sing on vowels and consonants that can be given pitch, as described in Peter Tkach's book, *Vocal Technique,* published by Neil A. Kjos. Beyond the basic techniques described by Tkach, jazz and pop singers learn how to create timbre changes in the voice by exaggerating diphthongs and triphongs. For example, "You are my sunshine" could be sung as "ee-u-oo are my-ee sun-sha-ee-ine." I have exaggerated to illustrate my point; however, the issue remains. Timbre changes can create meanings and emotions when used effectively. Jazz and pop singers can be taught how to produce timbre changes through aural imaging.

Listen to how the great artists do these things and practice them until these sounds become part of your vocal repertoire. If your technique is correct, you can produce many kinds of sounds without injuring your vocal mechanism.—DR

It cannot be too strongly emphasized that the jazz/show choir bases its standards of tone production, blend, and balance upon the same Western-European–derived choral practices found in the vast majority of American public school choral organizations. From this base of sound music making, all styles of American popular music are possible. The foundation stays the same; the styles are different. If you can, teach your choir to sound like at least half a dozen different choirs during the course of a performance.

Three of the greatest contributors to vocal abuse are excessive amplitude (yelling instead of singing), lack of sleep (particularly troublesome at summer music camps), and taking in too little air prior to beginning each phrase. It's easy to be lazy—fight the feeling!

One of the smartest things a choir director can do is to have as many of his or her students as possible take private voice lessons. Another effective strategy is to bring in outside clinicians or fellow teachers to work with your choir. The enrichment will be worth it, and it doesn't have to cost a lot of money.—KS

Chapter 4

Rehearsal Techniques

The First Rehearsal

At the first rehearsal, select music that will be successful fairly quickly. You can add the extra polish and zing that are needed later. Don't worry so much about announcements and other organizational things. Instead, start singing right away. Students always enjoy getting a number down quickly. Once they know the music, add movements.—SKA

Subsequent Rehearsals

If a jazz/show choir is new to you, please have no fear! The same vocal techniques that work for your concert choirs and madrigal groups will also work for your jazz and show ensembles. The only differences have to do with diction. My general rule is "Sing it like you speak it." This most often has to do with softening inner and final consonants, or using "stopped consonants" (your tongue moves quickly to the roof of your mouth—for example, "imploding" rather than "exploding" final Ts).

You should plan rehearsal time carefully, just as you would with your concert choir, programming a variety of activities and styles. As in any rehearsal, demand concentration, good vocal tone, and discipline. You, the director, must be organized and productive. Hard work on a song for ten to twelve minutes can be enough. I always try to end with a "sing-through" of the number to see which points I was trying to accomplish took hold and how much of the number has been memorized.

Try to plan some listening time within your rehearsals. Listening to other groups perform can always help your singers. Ask them to listen for a particular item—dynamics, articulation, diction, style, or blend. Groups to listen to include Manhattan Transfer, New York Voices, Singers Unlimited, Take Six, Fred Waring's Pennsylvanians and The King's Singers.

Many publishers offer accompaniment/performance cassettes for purchase. These can be helpful tools, especially when perfecting the dancing or when performing in locations without a tuned piano.—SKA

Ten Suggestions for Vocal Jazz Directors

1. Have a thorough knowledge of the music before the first rehearsal. You must know exactly how each note, chord, and har-

mony functions and how it should sound. I strongly recommend harmonic analysis of every piece of music you rehearse.

2. Select only the finest arrangements available. Gene Puerling, Phil Mattson, and Kirby Shaw are three arrangers who have published high-quality, challenging literature. The more you challenge yourself and your singers, the more musical growth you will experience in your ensemble. Incorporating theory in the rehearsal will transform your choir from "dumb singers" to "smart musicians."

3. Be sure your keyboard skills are adequate for rehearsal purposes.

4. Make your jazz/show ensemble a select ensemble; singing jazz is quite challenging. Incorporate this ensemble into your total choral program.

5. Listen critically to recordings of jazz groups and great jazz singers. Insist that your students listen, too.

6. Refine your rehearsal techniques to be the most efficient possible. Talk less, isolate problem spots, keep up the pace. Don't leave a mistake uncorrected, and always insist on 110 percent effort. Get away from the notes and make music!

7. Purchase a multiple-microphone sound system that incorporates close-microphone singing. Ideally, there should be no more than two people per mike.

8. Learn about the rhythm section (piano, bass, drums). Know the function of each instrument and be able to explain to your instrumentalists exactly what you want from them.

9. Don't be overly concerned with "special effects" such as glissandos and fall-offs. These are not as important as knowing the score and helping your singers sing each chord with the correct notes, blend, balance, and style.

10. Let the musical line and a thoughtful delivery of the lyric be your inspiration for interpretation, especially in ballads. Minimize vibrato, particularly with close harmonies. Encourage student creativity, especially with solo interpretation and vocal improvisation.

The most important point to realize is that there is essentially no difference in directing the vocal jazz ensemble and the traditional choral ensemble. The director must teach the music written on the page using traditional choral elements such as blend, balance, intonation, vowel unification, and diction.—SZ

Pizzaz

Establish the right atmosphere for your rehearsal. The success of the show-choir rehearsal can be based on one word: PIZZAZ.

P = positive mindset. A positive rehearsal will motivate the choir to be the best it can be. Remember, positivism generates positivism and negativism begets negativism.

I = intelligence. An excellent show choir will have intelligent singers that believe in having successful rehearsals. It is amazing that when a show choir becomes the "in" place to be, you discover that the overall G.P.A. of the ensemble is much above average.

Z = zip. The eyes of the singers must express zip and enthusiasm. When the performers' eyes sparkle, they convey excitement to the audience.

Z = zest. The smile of the singers must communicate zest. An important element of the show choir performance is the excitement and vitality of the smiles.

A = attitude. The choir must be open to new ideas and possess a desire to excel. An enthusiastic attitude is essential for an excellent show choir.

Z = zeal. You as the director must be a zealot if your choir is to excel. You need to stand up for your belief that the show choir is an important, beneficial ensemble.

Remember: your choir is a mirror of you, the director. If you are positive, intelligent, have zip in your eyes and zest in your smile, an enthusiastic attitude, and are a zealot, then you will have an outstanding rehearsal and ultimately an outstanding jazz/show choir.—RW

Warm-ups

Choral warm-ups should be of the same carefully planned, excellent quality for a jazz/show choir as those used for the concert choir. You must make sure that the voices are ready to sing well. Use warm-ups to correct problems in choral parts. The creative teacher writes new warm-ups to correct the problems rather than using the same mundane warm-ups day after day.

Warm up the students' minds as much as their voices. Students come to choir from many activities: some from physical education, some from a history exam, and some from a fight with a friend. Do innovative warm-ups to motivate the choir and capture the students' minds.—RW

Use warm-ups that apply to the music that will be rehearsed. Chordal warm-ups could include adding sevenths and ninths to chords, allowing your singers to be more aware of these tones and the tighter harmonies they produce.

Warm-ups get the voice and the ear working. Ask students to listen to the sounds you are presenting and to their balance and blend. Warm-ups also offer the director time to clean up any problems with vocal technique, as well as a way to prepare singers for a trouble spot in an upcoming selection.—SKA

Chapter 5

Styles   **Repertoire**

"Pop" is often considered a bad word in the choral music-education profession. There are many criticisms: pop lyrics are trite and often suggestive, singing pop can cause vocal abuse, some pop performers have questionable vocal skills and moral characters, and the decibel levels are painfully high, to name a few.

Certainly some of these criticisms are justified. However, the same American popular music scene (I refer to "pop" as any music that is appealing to ordinary persons, including jazz and Broadway, as well as Top Forty and all the rest) that spawns these criticisms also easily qualifies as the richest pop music culture the world has ever seen. What used to be primarily a white-dominated, Tin-Pan-Alley, pop music market has been forever enriched through the inclusion of African-American culture (blues, gospel, jazz, rhythm and blues, rock and roll, soul) along with an ever-growing blend of folk, country, Hispanic, Cajun, and other musics. Pop music may contain incredible rhythmic complexity, remarkable technological innovation, and subtleties of inflection and tone quality that defy written notation. These subjects are worthy of scholarly study and stylistic imitation.

What does all this mean to you as a beginning jazz/show choir director? First, all music is subjective. That is to say: there is good and bad in all kinds of music. Your task is to choose what music your choir should be singing. Start by finding a way to acquire stylistic authenticity in any style you wish your choir to sing and by being able to demonstrate that authenticity to your choir in the classroom. How? Imitation, imitation, imitation (the best "style" teacher there is).

Ask musicians you respect to recommend outstanding recordings of vocal style. Find those materials (borrow them, if necessary) and sing along (singing for fifteen minutes a day in your car with cassette tapes can do wonders). Master every note, every inflection, every rhythmic and phrasing subtlety. Your voice will be able to do things that you never thought possible.

There are plenty of artists who may inspire you to copy every sound they make. Don't plan on doing any Broadway pieces unless you've heard Liza Minelli (rent the video "Cabaret"); any black gospel music until you know Aretha Franklin's renditions; any jazz without admiring Carmen McRae and Sarah Vaughan; any scat singing without listening to Jon Hendricks and Ella Fitzgerald; or any blues without hearing B. B. King. A lot of music educators will tell you to listen, listen, listen. Take it one step further and don't stop until you can reasonably approximate a whole host of sounds that the great artists make on a regular basis. The better you can imitate, the better your teaching abilities will be. The best teachers are the ones who can "do it," not just talk about it. Make it your goal to be a "doer."

Vibrato is always a negotiable item in the jazz/show choir (more in Broadway and gospel, less in jazz and pop). A knowledge of inflections is crucial to the singing of jazz/show choir material. Most choral arrangements don't have inflection marks written in the score, so it's up to you to provide them. Most important, give yourself and your students permission to add inflections to the jazz/show choir music you perform.—KS

Jazz is an evolving art form. New jazz styles develop for a variety of reasons, but when a particular style has lasting value, it becomes part of the standard repertoire and remains with us. As vocal jazz directors and performers, we need to be familiar with all styles. Performance and improvisation should be consistent with the style of music being performed. The following styles make up most of the standard jazz repertoire.

- Swing: two-beat, straight ahead (four-beat), shuffle
- Latin: bossa nova, rhumba, samba, reggae
- Rock: shuffle rock, funk rock
- Bebop
- Gospel
- Ballads

When developing a library for the choir, it is a good idea to purchase several pieces from each category. Start with easy charts and work to more difficult arrangements. An easy chart performed very well is a much better choice for the performer and the listener.—DR

Selection

As you learn more about stylistic authenticity, you will be better equipped to judge the relative worth of the choral arrangements you choose. You'll avoid songs with trite lyrics and gravitate toward the standards. With your new knowledge of rhythmic subtlety you'll be able to spot arrangers who don't know how to incorporate it: the words won't flow smoothly. As you learn that jazz singers routinely change the given melody in delightful ways, you'll find yourself looking for arrangements that do the same. We're teaching kids about life through music; therefore, choose songs that uplift, not pull down.

One of the most neglected ways of finding worthwhile choral arrangements is by asking leaders in the field for their list of the top twenty-five Christmas pieces, graduation songs, barn-burner vocal jazz festival pieces, show-choir openers, a cappella ballads, spirituals, folk songs, madrigals, or whatever. As you attend workshops and conventions, you'll find wonderful human resources who may live thousands of miles away but are no farther away than a phone call. Don't be afraid to call those people whose pictures and names you see in music education journals. They will be glad to help you and will be grateful to you for helping them stay abreast of what's going on at the grass-roots level.—KS

In selecting repertoire, I try to choose the most challenging, high-quality literature that serves choral music education first; I also select a variety of styles that will appeal to a wide audience. One goal is to have everybody in the audience like, enjoy, or relate to something about the program.—SZ

Checklist for Selecting Music

- *Find a good music dealer*—one you can count on, who will send out copies on approval, whose taste is similar to yours, who sells music from all publishers, who has a choral buyer who knows the market, and who can get the music to you promptly.
- *Spend time listening to promotional tapes*—it's worth it. Even though you might only hear a minute of a song, you will stay up to date with the trends and hear the latest pop hits. Mark the titles you are interested in seeing full copies of, then call your music dealer.
- *Select a variety*—watch to make sure you don't have too many tunes in one style or one key. Also make sure that you have a variety of sounds.
- *Look for pieces by composers and arrangers whose work has been successful for you*—the good ones will tend to have variety within their work. Also ask your friends which composers and arrangers they have had the most success with.
- *Keep up with the latest*—it's okay to purchase the latest pop ballad or the hit theme song from the recent Disney animated film. Just don't choose all your music this way, or your library will be unusable in future years.
- *Choose classic standard arrangements*—find a few pieces that will live on in your library—great tunes like "42nd Street" or "Stormy Weather" will be crowd pleasers for years to come. Do your best to make sure these great standards stay alive!
- *Keep your ears open*—go to competitions, festivals, and concerts at neighboring schools. Be on the lookout for new material and ideas for pacing and programming a show.

- *Do not write your own arrangements*—unless the song has gone into the public domain (generally, one that was copyrighted more than seventy-five years ago). Arranging without permission is illegal. But feel free to adapt existing purchased arrangements that are in print by eliminating repeats, or combining two selections into a mini-medley, for example.—SKA

Buying Music on a Budget

If you're just starting out, aim high and try to find a teaching job in a school that supports music. If that fails, borrow music from other schools. If your school or district is currently suffering a cash crunch, pooling all of your district's music in a single location can help until things get better. There are a lot of schools who raise their own money for music purchases through various kinds of performance activities. A booster club of interested parents requires time and energy but can reap large benefits for the music program.—KS

Chapter 6

Accompaniment and Sound Equipment

Accompaniment

There is no substitute for live accompaniment. It is important for choral directors to develop a vocabulary and enough knowledge to relate well with an instrumental ensemble. If a rhythm section is not possible, prerecorded accompaniment tapes are available from several music publishers. Alternatively, with synthesizer and computer technologies available, accompaniments can be sequenced and an entire combo can "magically" be heard by pushing one button on one synthesizer!—SZ

Sound Equipment

I am a firm believer in using a sound system, specifically, a multiple-microphone system with as few singers as possible on each microphone. At my school, we have sixteen singers who sing directly into sixteen microphones. We developed this approach for three reasons:

- The individual singer will be challenged to achieve the best possible pitch, blend, intonation, and balance because his or her voice cannot hide; it will be on an equal basis with the other singers.
- The vocal instrument will be preserved. When using a microphone close to the mouth, the singer doesn't have to shout or strain the voice to be heard over the instrumental accompaniment.
- Contemporary technology includes microphones and sound systems; they are used in all aspects of professional music. This technology is here to stay. We do a disservice to our students if we don't teach them about microphone technique.

Although the purchase of sophisticated sound equipment can be very costly, and the setting up, tearing down, and maintenance can be quite time consuming, the musical development in you and your students is worth every ounce of effort.—SZ

For many choral directors, the sound system is the most problematic element of performance. To begin, refer to Doug Anderson's *Jazz and Show Choir Handbook, II* (Hinshaw Music)—it's loaded with solutions. Microphone use can range from none to a spread of four to six across the front of the stage to many microphones, with small groups or an individual on each one. The closer you sing into a mike, the more complex monitoring the sound gets and the more likely you'll need a sound technician (usually a gifted student from the audiovisual department) as part of your choir.

Balancing the voices can be a problem. A poorly adjusted sound system or one person standing too close to a microphone can destroy the balance or blend of your choir. If you plan to use a sound system in performances, try to use it at every rehearsal. Be sure to provide for tight security; it's easy for microphones to "disappear."

Sound systems have created a gulf between some more traditional choral directors, who resent what they feel is an unwarranted intrusion of technology into the natural sound of human voices, and other directors who enjoy the benefits of modern technology and the exciting possibilities a well-run sound system can bring to their choral experience. Before you decide to use a sound system, think about the pros and cons, and make your decision based on what you think is best for your choir, not on what some other choir is doing. Avoid trends of any kind unless they work for you and your choir.—KS

Chapter 7
Choreography

Choreography for a show choir is strictly the icing on the cake. Don't let the movement be too busy or active, or you will crumble the cake! Be tasteful and have fun. Remember that singers need to breathe deeply, so don't heavily choreograph every selection. Even within one number, plan for some sections to have more movement while others have less.

For the jazz choir, you may wish to plan organized, simple movements here and there, but staying close to microphones is usually the first priority. Add movement with hands, arms, shoulders, or knees to accent vocal articulations or interesting rhythms.

Ballads are often left alone, in terms of movement. You can design a "tableau" or picture on stage using levels or stools. Risers, platforms, and boxes add variety to your stage picture and enable all of your singers to been seen easily by you and the audience.—SKA

Checklist for Choreography

- *Theme*—come up with a theme or main concept for each number.
- *Key lyrics*—pick out your favorite movement-oriented words, ones that may suggest an activity to you. Usually, I select one word per musical phrase for beginning groups.
- *Rhythms and rests*—look in the vocal lines and in the piano part for interesting rhythms and rests. Accent these with movement.
- *Position of singers*—give each number its own look. Clusters, circles, partners, trios, straight lines, a bowling pin formation, a semicircle—all these are possible.
- *Simplicity and variety*—keep your movements simple and clean, and add variety by changing direction or having different groups do the same movement at different times. If the chorus repeats, repeat the movement that accompanies it.
- *Facial work*—make certain the students say with their faces what they are saying with their mouths. Work on eye contact and focus as well as keeping the mouth facing front.
- *Style*—be familiar with moves that work well in the style of the piece, whether it's jazz, hot rock, soft shoe, or country.
- *Vocal considerations*—don't choreograph movements that will adversely affect the choral sound. Consider featuring two or three couples doing movement in front of the ensemble if you feel the vocals are loosing strength.
- *Upper torso vs. footwork*—keep movements above or around the

head as much as possible. Fancy footwork is fun, but it may take away from the vocals, so wait until you have an interlude or dance break.

- *Props/costume additions*—try the unexpected: choreograph puppets, use white gloves with black light, try movement with beach towels or flashlights. Add a hat or bandanna, a vest or an apron.—SKA

For Beginners

If you are a beginner, go get help! Try a summer camp or workshop, or check out sessions at conventions. Observe festivals and competitions. Check out the theme parks and old movie musicals. Gather ideas and inspiration anywhere you can.

Your students may be a wonderful resource, but be careful that they aren't trying to do too much within one song. You could call the nearest college director who has a show choir; there may be a talented student lurking there who could give you a hand.

Write down your movement ideas in the octavo—I suggest using a red or blue pencil so that you can see it easily. Write down rhythms if it will help, or use stick figures. Then, when you think you have it all figured out, make sure you can do it backwards, mirroring the students!—SKA

When Should I Use Choreography?

I was once asked: "Where do you draw the line in doing choreography with your choirs?" I had to pause for a minute but quickly realized that first of all, it serves very little purpose to draw such lines and, second, there is nothing in the visual medium of choral music that should not be at least staged if not fully choreographed. (I almost did tell the inquirer that I probably would not choreograph Handel's "Hallelujah Chorus" but quickly remembered that the king himself stood up, obviously with the intention of moving to the music.) On a more serious note, experts agree and studies have shown that 70 percent of what audiences go home remembering from any live performance is what they have seen.

This can be disheartening for a choral conductor whose priority is to produce beautiful, emotional, even inspirational sounds. But it does suggest that ignoring 70 percent of what your audience is taking in is at best insensitive and maybe at some level self-serving. If you invite an audience to come out of their homes and sit through your concerts, you owe it to them to make the adventure as visually appealing as you will assuredly make it aurally thrilling. Otherwise, you may as well just send them CDs and coupons for take-out food.

Now this may sound militant and even radical, but in truth it's really quite ordinary. You have always staged your performances, even in your most traditional concert settings. You have had your choir members walk in single file onto four rickety risers in their purple choir robes and yellow stoles, turn to face you as you made your grand entrance, and stand for the entire concert with hands held reservedly at their sides or nervously in front of them.

What perhaps you didn't realize was that the instant you gave the command to your choir to "Walk out there, stand still, look at me, and sing," you committed yourself to being a staging director as well as a conductor of great music. Every direction that you gave them was a staging choice. Then as you began to get a bit more specific ("Put your feet together with your downstage foot a little closer to the audience so more people can fit on the risers, and don't pinch your neighbor"), you began to understand how even the smallest details could make your concerts more visually rewarding, with no cost to your vocal priority!

In fact, you will probably discover that your choir sings with more discipline, more concentration, and even more musicality because of your attention and tasteful staging directions. It's true that many times the most effective staging will involve no movement at all. But it is important to realize that even the choice to stand perfectly still is a staging choice.—JJ

Where Do I Start?

This is a loaded question. If you think that staging or directing a jazz or show choir can be summed up in a few pages, you are kidding yourself. If you think that you can work for twelve weeks on an octavo, make certain that each musical nuance is precise, and then throw in a few moves the night before the performance and expect a quality show, you need to reconsider. Choreography and staging even at the beginning levels are hard work!

Nothing breeds enthusiasm and self-confidence like quick success. For your first forays into choreography, try something that you are absolutely sure everybody in the group will be able to master with a minimum amount of time. For example, use a song that everybody knows such as "America the Beautiful," and add some arm movements to the chorus. (Raise your right arm on the first "America," then scoop your left arm on the second "America" so that both arms are overhead. Clasp hands together (over your head) on the word "God." Open your hands and let them drop slowly toward your audience and to your sides on the words "shed his grace on thee" as though you are tossing "grace" onto your listeners. Hold hands in long lines on the word "brotherhood" and raise those held hands overhead during the end of the refrain, "from sea to shining sea.") You will notice that the choreography, although simple, is reflective of both the musical line and the lyric. Choreography that reflects neither one of these should be reexamined. Consider that the move for "God" was a clasping of the hands overhead as though you were praying. See how you suggest brotherhood to the audience by holding hands in long lines on that lyric.

Adding choreography to your music need not be intimidating. Start simply and move on from there. What you will quickly realize is that the very best choreography simply enhances the message or musicality of each selection. More often than not, the success of the movement lies entirely on the commitment of the performers to execute it with enthusiastic sincerity. Holding your hands to your chest as you sing the word "me" and then reaching to your audience when you sing "you" many seem trite at first examination. But, if performed with enthusiasm, it is very often the perfect move for that lyric. The key is that the performer must be well prepared and totally committed to each move, just as he or she is committed to the musical aspects of the performance.

As a new staging director/choreographer, you will be surprised at how your own "bag of tricks" grows as you get more involved in choreography. Just like a vocal director who attends regular choral workshops collects vocal warm-ups and conducting techniques to utilize with his or her singers, the budding choreographer who keeps an open mind and eye will build a vocabulary and repertoire on which to base creative endeavors.

You do not have to have had dance training since childhood in order to make wonderful contributions to the visual side of your concerts and shows. In fact, the best choreographers are very often those with a strong background in choral music with some experience in movement.

Do not be afraid to let your students make contributions to the visual aspects of the show. Set yourself up as the producer who has veto power, but encourage their input in both the design and teaching of the staging for some or all of the concert. After all, the choir is a situation for learning and should be a laboratory for them to be involved in as many facets of the process as possible.

Be wary of enlisting the help of the local dance teacher or cheerleading adviser and giving him or her free reign to stage your jazz or show choir. Despite their good intentions, such people may not have any experience in vocal music. This is just a friendly reminder to be alert and not give up your rights to adjust and delete in order to keep the quality of the musical performance as high as possible.

I can't tell you everything to do and not to do with movement when starting a jazz/show choir. In fact, we do ourselves a disservice if we presume that this is an art form that is already defined; it still very new. Jazz/Show choirs are great art forms that are not here to replace anything that you have been doing in other musical venues. They are simply another option in the dynamic world of choral music.

Because I can't tell you everything, I'll just offer ten tips that have worked for me. Take them for what they are worth, and then get yourself to a workshop!—JJ

Nine "Do's" and One "Don't" for Staging a Performance

■ *Do* consider that every single song requires staging! Some numbers may consist of standing in four rows on the risers, one foot slightly forward toward the conductor, period. If it is followed by a number that includes sixty-four bars of lambada music and inflatable dancing palm trees, you need to make different staging choices. It does matter what you look like at all times.

■ *Do* experiment with having a different look for each selection. You may choose to perform two or three songs in succession without changing your formation. But this should be the exception. Even if you simply have every other person move a step forward so that four rows become eight rows for the next selection, you've given your audiences a new sensation to enjoy without sacrificing anything from your vocal priority. Maybe for the third number the lines could switch so that different faces are in front. It's an easy way to spice up your program visually.

■ *Do* be willing to take the risk of doing choreography with your large ensembles. In many ways it is easier to do movement with a lot of people as opposed to just a few. If ten singers do a single move, it often doesn't look like much happened, and it may not be worth the effort. However, the same move executed by one hundred performers can be very impressive. In this instance "more is better."

■ *Do* rehearse everything that will be presented to your audience, including bows, transitions, entrances, exits, and even your behavior as the conductor. Even things that you want to appear spontaneous should be thought out and rehearsed before you subject the audience to them. Using the old line "I'll get into it when the audience is out there" is unprofessional and insulting to your fans, who deserve your very best.

■ *Do* encourage ambitious members of your choir to come up with ideas for staging the entire group themselves. It's a wonderful part of the creative process for them and allows you to step out of the role of choreographer and into the role of producer. Do not be afraid to modify their ideas to suit your tastes and mature analytical skills.

Remember, your students are just learning and require your guidance. Have students explain their ideas to you before they present them to the entire cast.

■ *Do* analyze the unique qualities of your cast members. Do you have a juggler, a magician, an acrobat, a ballerina, a ventriloquist, or a buffoon? Can the tallest girl perform as a partner to the smallest guy? Can the senior boys do a number all by themselves? That's entertainment!

■ *Do* layer your choreography so that seldom is everyone dancing full out at the same time; that is too demanding on the singers and on the eyes of the audience. Too much movement or too much standing still is like too much ice cream: after four bowls of Chocolate Revel, it almost doesn't taste good anymore.

■ *Do* vary the amount of choreography from song to song. For example, try having everybody incorporate some movement in the first song, with perhaps a third of the group moving on the second, nobody moving on the third piece, and everybody moving again on the fourth. It seems a bit obvious, but now you've added visual interest to your musical selections.

■ *Do* read Fritz Mountford's book *The Art of Entertainment*. It is full of useful ideas for choirs of all styles and levels of experience. I'm certain that it will soon be required reading for all serious directors of choral music.

■ *Don't* be intimidated or resistant to "things they never taught you at the school of emerging choral conductors." We work in a wonderfully dynamic art form. We'll never know it all or master even most of it. Thank goodness!—JJ

How Do I Learn?

Imagine what it would be like if a doctor graduated from medical school, began to practice, and never read another journal or took another class in new techniques in the field. It would not be tolerated. Similarly, there is no excuse now for not learning more about building and staging a jazz/show choir. There are countless workshops and camps of varying lengths and concentrations dedicated precisely to this art form, especially in the summer. Some are directed toward young students, some toward teachers, and some to both. Many are available for college credit. Most have some sort of culminating performance, and almost all are worth your time. Nobody's going to take you by the hand and lead you to the workshops; you must take the initiative. Once you are there, however, understanding professionals will lead you through a nonthreatening course that will make you a better producer. Check choral journals and newsletters for information on a workshop that will serve your needs. Go once, and I promise you'll be hooked.

Watch MTV. Go to festivals and concerts where the choirs use choreography and borrow ideas. Go to a dance hall, line-dance party, a dance class, a Broadway-style show, or a video store to pique your creativity. Don't be intimidated. You can do this and all that you've done so well in the past.—JJ

Chapter 8
Shows, Concerts, and Festivals

Programming

When determining the show my group will perform, I consider many elements—miniconcerts for civic organizations, festivals, full concerts for the public, the ages of my audiences, students' desires, and the educational value of particular performances. If there is a consistency to my programs, it is variety through different eras. It is important for teenagers to experience all musics. Educationally it is important for them to see and hear the musical difference in time periods and to understand the relationship of music to its ethnic or historical context.

I allow my students to choose two or three numbers; usually they select tunes they are familiar with. That gives them a vested interest in the performance. I then fill out the rest of the program with music from the past and present from several genres. Several genres can be performed in a single concert if properly arranged and introduced.

I choose the entire program for festivals. If I classify my ensemble as a jazz ensemble, I choose exclusively jazz or blues. If I classify my ensemble as a show choir, I may do a variety of styles, including jazz. In any case, I want my students to be challenged and to present a well-prepared program.

I always start my program with an upbeat, choreographed number; this lets students harness the nervous energy that usually accompanies adjudication events. I begin up, and I end up, even if I return to the opening number as my closing selection.

When developing a show for a festival program, I try to choose music that is challenging and requires great effort of the students. I choose a piece that allows my group to showcase its ability to dance while singing, and I also choose a number that showcases the most important part of the ensemble— singing. This number usually falls in the middle of the program and is performed in a block or still, staged formation. It is usually slow and, when possible, a capella.

For festival purposes, I avoid the novelty pieces. They may fit well into a performance at home, but I advise against them for adjudicated events. As a general rule, I prefer contrasting genres and tempos, with each selection providing a particular challenge to the choir as well as an element to showcase.

One other element of programming I consider regardless of the type of performance is the text. Fortunately, the arrangers of show choir music do a wonderful job of choosing music that avoids controversial subjects. Even so, always study the text yourself to determine its appropriateness.

To go one step further, try to choose at least one number that has a message of peace or hope or that exhibits a positive thought. Show choirs should be goodwill ambassadors, and nothing will sell your performance better than hearing students sing a number of this nature. When young people demonstrate and express a positive theme or thought, they will win a place in the hearts of their audience.

To summarize my philosophy and practice in programming: use a variety of styles and genres, contrast tempos from song to song, allow for choreography within the singing and dancing abilities of students, keep the program educational and challenging, and keep it positive and clean.—GM

Michael Cesario, who teaches theatre at the State University of New York–Purchase, talks about the three most important ingredients of a successful program:

- *Tradition*—if something is dear to your group, keep singing it. If your choir has a traditional ballad, sing it. If your school has a tradition of great choral groups, fight to save it!
- *Innovation*—keep looking for new ideas and inspiration. Keep things moving forward within your program. Come up with new ways to do things.
- *State of the art*—keep up with what's happening in the school choral scene. Know what the publishers have to offer and what their top sellers are. Who are the leaders in the choral field today? What are they doing out there?

Putting together a show can be the most exciting thing you do—starting with the selection of the right material for your group. Make sure that your students understand why you have selected each piece. Aim for a variety of emotions, tempos, textures, keys, eras, and styles.—SKA

A Possible Show—Fifteen to Twenty Minutes

- *Opener*—hot, up-tempo, flashy movement.
- *Swing tune*—slick, cooler tempo, showing off tight vocal sound (may be choreographed).
- *Novelty number*—highly staged, so the audience will laugh with you.
- *Mini-medley*—featuring an era, a topic, or an artist; combine two to four songs, perhaps one that features a solo or duet; some choreography.
- *Ballad*—sentimental, perhaps a cappella.
- *Closer*—higher emotion than the opener or the ballad; fast, fun, full-sounding—leave the audience wanting more!—SKA

The Festival Experience

I recommend going to festivals and competitions. Don't go just to win, but go to be the best you can be, to cheer on other groups, and to learn from watching them.

Make sure you take a look at the judging sheet before you go. It helps to know what the judges will be evaluating. Different judges will have different opinions. When adjudication is given by tape, listen to the judges' comments alone before sharing them with the students. Give yourself time to absorb what the judges are saying so that you may better prepare your students for the judges' comments. Consider their suggestions as ideas for growth in your group. Some comments may be helpful and eye-opening, other may reinforce things you have been saying all year.

Prepare your students for a positive experience—and have a great time forming the bond that develops when choral ensembles travel and sing together!

Your jazz/show choir should be an extension of your total program, not the main focus. Make an effort to travel and put on concerts with all of your choirs—it may be a challenge for you, but your total program will see the benefits in the long run.—SKA

Chapter 9
Administration

Organization

How does one organize a jazz/show choir? The answer is very simple. An excellent show choir uses the same organization as an excellent concert choir but adds choreography. To organize a jazz/show choir, you should follow eleven steps.

1. First, obtain permission from the administration. Always keep the administration informed of your activities with the choir, and publicly acknowledge the administration members for their assistance in creating the ensemble.

2. Establish a budget and follow it.

3. Find excellent new literature. Just as you would find outstanding selections for the concert choir, you will also need to find excellent literature for the jazz/show choir. Five ways you may find this literature are: attend music company reading sessions, contact major publishers for demonstration tapes, attend university classes on choral literature emphasizing jazz/show choirs, attend jazz/show choir festivals, and attend summer jazz/show choir camps and workshops.

4. Select outfits. The selection of the proper outfit can be one of the biggest headaches. Select an outfit that is proper for the age of the singers, within the financial abilities of the singers, and flattering to singers of all sizes. I recommend that you consult with another jazz/show choir director to find out what works best. Some outfits look great in a picture or when the choir is standing still, but they may restrict the choreographed movement.

5. Work with the booster club. Meet with the booster club (if one is recognized by the school) and outline its responsibilities. A booster club can be a tremendous asset or an unbearable detriment. You and the administration must make sure that a booster club's constitution is within the boundaries of the school district's policies. A booster club can help raise funds, serve as a sponsor for trips to festivals and contests, make props, and make outfits. The booster club members should not make musical decisions or personnel decisions.

6. Schedule rehearsal time. If the jazz/show choir is scheduled to rehearse outside of the school day or if additional rehearsals are needed, examine the school schedule to find best time for rehearsals. If the choir only meets outside of school time, make

sure that the choir doesn't dominate the student's free time. If this occurs, you may lose some of your best students, because they are often involved in many school activities.

7. Plan concerts, festivals, and competitions. Many of the finest high school jazz/show choirs have all concerts, festivals, and competitions planned before the school year beings. This helps everyone involved to avoid possible conflicts with other events. Remember not to overbook your choir.

8. Schedule transportation. The jazz/show choir director must schedule transportation to all festivals and competitions in accordance with school district rules.

9. Audition choir members. Advertise audition dates throughout the school. To ensure selecting the finest choir members, you must promote the auditions. If you have made the jazz/show choir the "in" place to be, there will be a large number of students auditioning.

10. Audition the accompanist and back-up ensemble. The jazz/show choir will need some type of accompanying ensemble. Discuss this selection with the instrumental director, thus eliminating any conflicts of double usage of students. Be sure all band members understand what is expected of them, including when they are required to rehearse and perform.

11. Select/hire a choreographer. Find someone who has the same views of musical importance as you do. Both you and the choreographer must agree on the difficulty of the movements and on the importance of the vocal sound. Call the director of a university jazz/show choir and request names of students who would be qualified to choreograph for your ensemble. Many music education students would love to share their expertise and also enhance their teaching techniques by working with your high school students.—RW

Another Method of Organization

All too often we music educators sequester ourselves in our rooms and schedules. Once we get a request for a performance, we retreat to the rehearsal hall not to be seen again until the performance. If we keep this up, we may miss the best opportunity to gain support for our programs.

An administrator usually doesn't prevent the development of a program unless it costs money or creates internal problems for him or her. Once you have created the opportunity to start a show choir, you are eventually going to have needs. It therefore behooves you to develop not only approval but support from everyone who will be associated with your program. The show choir is the perfect opportunity to build such support for your entire choral program. Building this support system requires careful planning.

First, your students must buy into your plans. This is the easiest step. It will be up to you to keep the students focused and continually working toward excellence. Second, once your students are ready, solicit opportunities to perform in the community. You should have a repertoire that will satisfy many audiences of many ages. Community groups, garden clubs, and local service clubs are perfect opportunities to market your jazz/show choir. Take several parent chaperons along. Seeing their children perform and hearing the positive remarks from the audiences are worthwhile for you and the parents.

Another opportunity to market both yourself and your ensemble is within the school classrooms. This works particularly well in history, humanities, and even literature classes. Perform for a history class a tune from the period they are studying. Perhaps your choir could sing a madrigal and then a pop number to show the some different forms of recreational music through history. This is entertaining as well as educational for both students and teachers.

Solicit letters from your audiences and have them sent to your administrators and local newspaper. Once this type of correspondence starts showing up on the desk of the principal and in letters to the editor, you will see pride, interest, and support begin to grow.

Organizing a show choir isn't much different from organizing a concert choir, except that the music may dictate different instrumentation, the use of choreography, or the employment of a sound reinforcement system. Approach rehearsals with the same determination you have for the concert choir. And your expectations should not be lower than those for your concert choir.

There are small differences between organizing a concert choir and organizing a jazz/show choir; let's consider them in detail.

The first consideration: what type of jazz/show choir do you want to establish? Is it going to be exclusively jazz? Perhaps you will build on Broadway themes, or maybe you will stay in the pop genre. Maybe you want to combine several styles—pop arrangements may be here one year, then out of print the next. If you have the budget and find a chart you like but don't necessarily have the student resources to perform it, buy the music anyway for future use. It may not be available by the time your students are capable of performing it.

Once you have decided the nature of your ensemble, determine how large or small you would like the group to be. If I'm doing Broadway or pop, where I employ choreography, I like a group of at least sixteen singers, four on each vocal part. Twenty-four is the largest group I have had, but you may have the facilities and resources to go even larger. If I'm doing jazz or gospel, I use a smaller group, usually six to eight singers. In any case, if you are just starting out, I suggest no less than three on a voice part. This helps develop confidence among singers and protects against a member missing a rehearsal or performance.

Next, plan which songs to choreograph. Keep it simple at first and concentrate on quality singing. A group can be impressive by singing well. But the best dancing can not cover up or hide poor musicianship.—GM

Grading

The grading of a jazz/show choir should be based on carefully selected criteria. Many teachers use the same criteria for both the concert choir and the jazz/show choir, because these teachers use the same tonal concepts in developing both of their choirs.

Adhere to school policy on grading. See if you can include concert attendance as a grading criterion. Positive attitude and pride in the choir will encourage an "A" grade. Here is a possible grading system for a jazz/show choir:

- *For an "A,"* a student must consistently participate in all classroom activities, have choral selections and choreography learned/memorized at the specified time, demonstrate much leadership ability and/or cooperation within the choir, display a positive attitude, and always obey the established classroom rules.
- *For a "B,"* a student must consistently participate in most classroom activities, usually have choral selections and choreography learned/memorized at the specified time, demonstrate some leadership ability and/or cooperation within the choir, display a better than average attitude, and usually obey the established classroom rules.
- *For a "C,"* a student must participate in more than half of classroom activities, often have choral selections and choreography learned/memorized at the specified time, demonstrate occasional leadership and/or cooperation within the choir, display an average attitude, and generally obey the established classroom rules.
- *For a "D,"* the student must participate in some classroom activities, rarely have choral selections and choreography learned/memorized at the specified time, demonstrate little leadership and/or cooperation within the choir, display a less than average attitude, and seldom obey the established classroom rules.—RW

Talent is not dispensed in equal portions. Therefore, do not grade according to talent. To keep it simple, base your grades on work ethics, daily participation, steady improvement, and participation in extra rehearsals and performances. Students start each grading period at "0" and work their way up. Consider whether students are grasping stylistic characteristics and are able to produce these characteristics in rehearsal and performance. If a student displays a strong work ethic on a daily basis, he or she will learn and improve. You can apply this to more detailed areas such as vocal techniques, reading skills, concepts of balance and blend and intonation, as well as many other musical features. Organize your class routine to provide time for skills and written exams, so you can get a feel for where your students are and determine where they need to be at the end of each grading period.—GM

Chapter 10

Outfits

What a dilemma—what should the jazz/show choir wear? The key aspects for me are that the costume be simple, fun, elegant, long-lasting, nonwrinkle, easy to move in, comfortable, sweat-absorbent, and appropriate for the age-group.

I recommend staying away from too much white—the light is then attracted to the clothing rather than to the singers' faces. It's always fun to have bright colors on stage, yet black is also effective. The first outfits the gals in my show choir wore were simple black jumpsuits from J. C. Penney's (in 1978). They were loose-fitting and gave me the option to add colorful blouses and jackets over the top. The men wore light yellow tux shirts with black pants.

Lately, at show choir festivals or camps, I've enjoyed using brightly colored polo shirts (or T-shirts) with tan or khaki pants of the students' choosing (jeans are fine, as long as there are no tears). Another group I conduct wears bright outfits of their choosing—no pastels, white, black, brown, or navy. Try using the colors of the rainbow. Another trick is to select certain colors, for instance, red, white, and black, and let singers wear whatever combination of those colors they choose (although I insist that the guys be more creative than white shirts and black pants). You do not need to spend a lot of money on costumes, although you may be able to get a more professional look if you do.

Since upper torso movement is used with lots of hand motions, you should make sure that clothing is rather loose around the arms. Men often have trouble with their shirt tails falling out, so you may wish to add a vest, sweater, or cummerbund.

Here are a few other tips. Limit jewelry and make sure that hair is neatly arranged so that it doesn't cover up the face. Buy comfortable, supportive shoes that match the outfit. Feel free to add a touch of sparkle with sequins around a hem or shirt collar.

There really are no rules to costuming, other than to use good taste. Your selection should reflect the image you are trying to portray, and it will depend on the age of your performers, financial considerations, travel schedule, locations at which you are performing, and the bodies you have to work with.—SKA

Buy Them, Make Them?

Well, I suppose that depends on your economic situation. Remember this: you cannot cover up bad music and lousy choreography with fancy costumes, scenery, and special effects. Keep your priorities straight! More sequins will not make your group sound better.

The first consideration for a costume is: "Is it appropriate?" Does it flatter everyone in the group? Do the young people in the choir still look like young people, or have I made them into Las Vegas–style show dancers? Will the costumes last from performance to performance with realistic upkeep expectations? Are the costumes versatile enough to accommodate a variety of styles of music and performance situations? Can we wear them for the Rotary Club Christmas program and for the all-school assembly? Can a simple change (e.g., a scarf, vest, jacket, or hat) change the costume enough to give it added versatility? Will I get phone calls from my performers' parents wondering what planet I flew in from? Or wondering when the "rest" of the costume is going to arrive? Can the performers "move" in the costumes, or are the skirts, pants, vests, or jackets too tight, too loose, too long, too short? Do the performers have the proper underwear—deodorant, dance pants, bras, and dance belts? You do them a favor when you speak openly and honestly about such essentials.

It is almost always a bad idea to have a few of the cast members get together, go to a mall, and decide on a costume. You are the producer. Their input may be helpful, but spare yourself and them the embarrassment of choosing an inappropriate costume that looks good on a mannequin or magazine cover but flatters nobody in your cast.

Keep in mind that the old show-business adage "less is more" is probably never more true than when choosing costumes for a jazz/show choir.—JJ

Selected Resources

Jay Althouse and Russell L. Robinson, *Developing Technique through Jazz/Pop Styles* (Alfred)
SATB, #11393
SAB, #11394
SoundTrax cassette, #11868

Doug Anderson, *Jazz and Show Choir Handbook* (Hinshaw)
330-page book plus CD, #HMB188

Kirby Shaw, *Junior Jazz* (Hal Leonard)
Two-Part Collection, #08666065
ShowTrax cassette, #08666066

Kirby Shaw, *Vocal Jazz Style* (Hal Leonard)
Manual, #08665580
SATB Singer's Edition, #08665581
Demonstration cassette, #08665582

Choreography Resources

Sally K. Albrecht, *Choral Music in Motion, Volume 1: Adding Movement to Your Choral Program* (Alfred: #2-102)

Sally K. Albrecht, *Choral Music in Motion, Volume 2: Movement for Larger Groups* (Alfred: #2-107)

John Jacobson, various videos and booklets available from Hal Leonard Publishing Corporation

Publishers

Alfred Publishing Company
PO Box 10003
16380 Roscoe Boulevard
Van Nuys, CA 91410

CPP/Belwin, Inc.
15800 NW 48th Avenue
PO Box 4340
Miami, FL 33014-9969

Hal Leonard Publishing Corporation
7777 W. Bluemound Road
Milwaukee, WI 53213

Kimmel Publications
380 South Main Place
Carol Stream, IL 60188

Plymouth Music Company
170 NE 33rd Street
PO Box 24330
Ft. Lauderdale, FL 33334

Shawnee Press
Delaware Water Gap, PA 18327

University of Northern Colorado Jazz Press
School of Music—Jazz Studies
Greeley, CO 80631

Acknowledgments

Russell L. Robinson, editor, is associate professor of music, codirector of the Chamber Singers at the University of Florida, and will become president of the Florida Music Educators Association in 1995. Robinson has been a clinician and conductor for more than a hundred festivals, workshops, and honor choirs throughout the United States, Canada, and Europe. Robinson is a published author in music education, as well as a choral composer and arranger who has published with MENC, CPP/Belwin, Plymouth Music, and Alfred Publishing Company.

Sally K. Albrecht (SKA) is the director of school choral publications for Alfred Publishing Company. She is a popular choral conductor and clinician, and she is especially known for her work with choral movement. Albrecht is a composer and the author of two books on choral movement: *Choral Music in Motion, Volumes 1 and 2*, distributed by Alfred. Her "We Are the Children" was performed at the 1994 MENC "World's Largest Concert," involving more than eight million singers. She has worked with thousands of teachers and students at clinics, conventions, and workshops in thirty-eight states and Canada.

John Jacobson (JJ), music educator and choreographer, is the president and founder of America Sings!, a nonprofit charitable organization, and he has served as a guest clinician at the Fred Waring Summer Choral Workshop, the Show Choir Camps of America, and Duke University's Brightleaf Music Workshop. Jacobson conducts his own seminars, workshops, and festivals for students and music educators as a freelance entertainment consultant. He is nationally recognized as an inspirational motivator of music teachers and students.

Gary Miller (GM) is director of choral activities at Vero Beach High School, Vero Beach, Florida. His choirs have been highly acclaimed in the state of Florida and at the International Choir Festival in Vienna, Austria. He is the jazz/show choir chair for the Florida Chapter of the American Choral Directors and district chair for the Florida Vocal Association.

Dave Riley (DR) is chair of music education and director/arranger for the Ithaca Vocal Jazz Ensemble at Ithaca College in New York. The Ithaca Vocal Jazz Ensemble has provided training experience for many jazz educators and performers, including the internationally acclaimed jazz ensemble, New York Voices. His work is published by

Alfred, CPP/Belwin, Kendor Music, Music 70/80, Cherry Lane Music, and Cambiata Press.

Kirby Shaw (KS) is a pioneer in the jazz choir movement and one of America's most prolific composers and arrangers of jazz/show choir music. He is a jazz singer who has "scatted" with such notables as Bobby McFerrin, Al Jarreau, Jon Hendricks, and Mark Murphy. As a conductor, clinician, and teacher, he has shared his expertise at all levels here and abroad.

Richard Weymuth (RW) is director of choirs at Northwest Missouri State University, Maryville, Missouri. He directs Northwest Celebration (a show choir), Tower Choir (a concert choir), and Madraliers (a madrigal ensemble). Weymuth has conducted more than five hundred festivals and workshops, including all-state choirs and major festivals in twenty-three states. He is the past president of the Missouri chapter of the American Choral Directors Association.

Stephen Zegree (SZ) is a professor of music at Western Michigan University, where he teaches piano and jazz, performs with the Western Jazz Quartet, and conducts Gold Company, an internationally recognized jazz/show vocal ensemble. The winner of numerous competitions, awards, and honors, Zegree is in demand as a guest conductor, pianist, clinician, and adjudicator around the world. His choral arrangements have been published by Hal Leonard, Jenson, and Shawnee Press, and he has recorded several demonstration tapes for Hal Leonard and Shawnee Press.

MENC's
Getting Started
Series

Each book in this series provides an outline to help new teachers, or teachers beginning new positions, gain confidence as they get started.

Getting Started with High School Band. By David S. Zerull. 1994. 52 pages. Stock #1627. ISBN 1-56545-045-0.

Getting Started with High School Choir. By Steven K. Michelson. 1994. 64 pages. Stock #1628. ISBN 1-56545-046-9.

Getting Started with Jazz Band. By Lissa A. Fleming. 1994. 64 pages. Stock #1626. ISBN 1-56545-035-3.

Getting Started with Jazz/Show Choir. Edited by Russell L. Robinson. 1994. 52 pages. Stock #1630. ISBN 1-56545-044-2.

Getting Started with Middle Level Band. By David G. Reul. 1994. 80 pages. Stock # 1631. ISBN 1-56545-049-3.

For information on these and other MENC publications, write to:

MENC Publications Sales
1806 Robert Fulton Drive
Reston, VA 22091-4348
Credit card holders may call 1-800-828-0229.